ARLO AND ZOE

DEDICATED TO: ALL KIDS AND GROWN UPS LEARNING TO TALK ABOUT THEIR EMOTIONS.

IT'S THE FIRST DAY OF SCHOOL
AND ZUG CANNOT WAIT!

ZUG WILL SEE FRIENDS.
ISN'T THIS GREAT!?

THEY WILL HOLD HANDS, HUG,
AND GIVE HIGH FIVES.

ZUG WANTS TO GET IN THE CAR
AND DRIVE!

IT'S ALSO ARLO'S FIRST DAY OF
SCHOOL!

ARLO WILL SEE FRIENDS,
ISN'T THIS COOL?

THEY WILL DRAW, PLAY CATCH,
AND HAVE TIME TO TALK.

ARLO RUNS TO THEIR PARENTS
AND SAYS "LET'S WALK!"

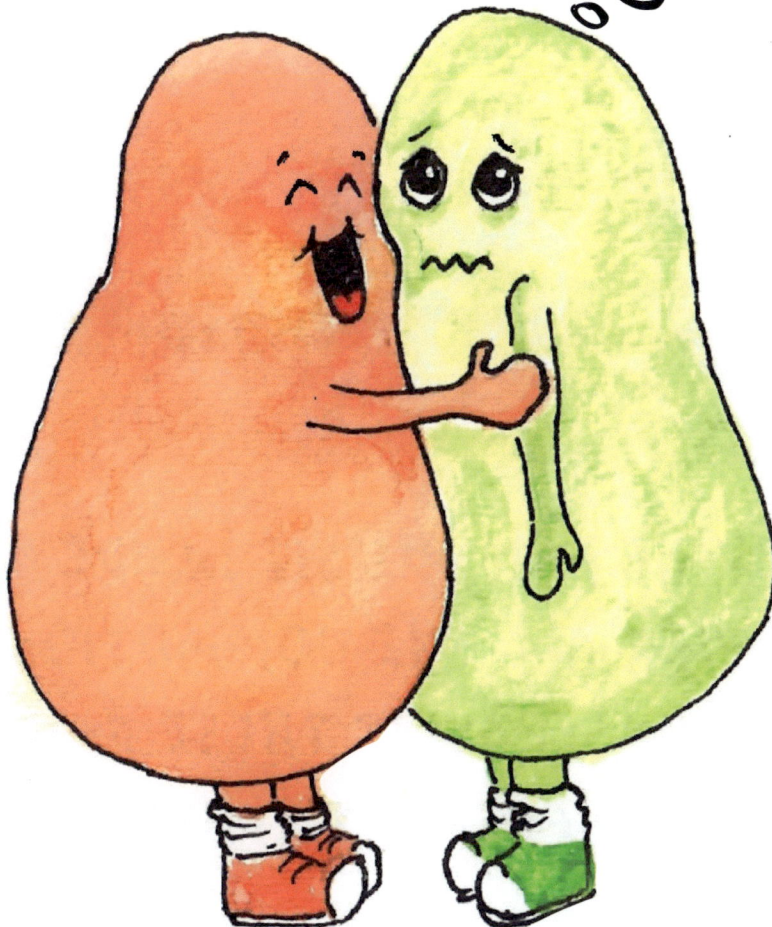

THE FRIENDS SIT INSIDE
AFTER ALL THE COMMOTION.
CAN YOU SEE THAT THESE FRIENDS
FEEL DIFFERENT EMOTIONS?

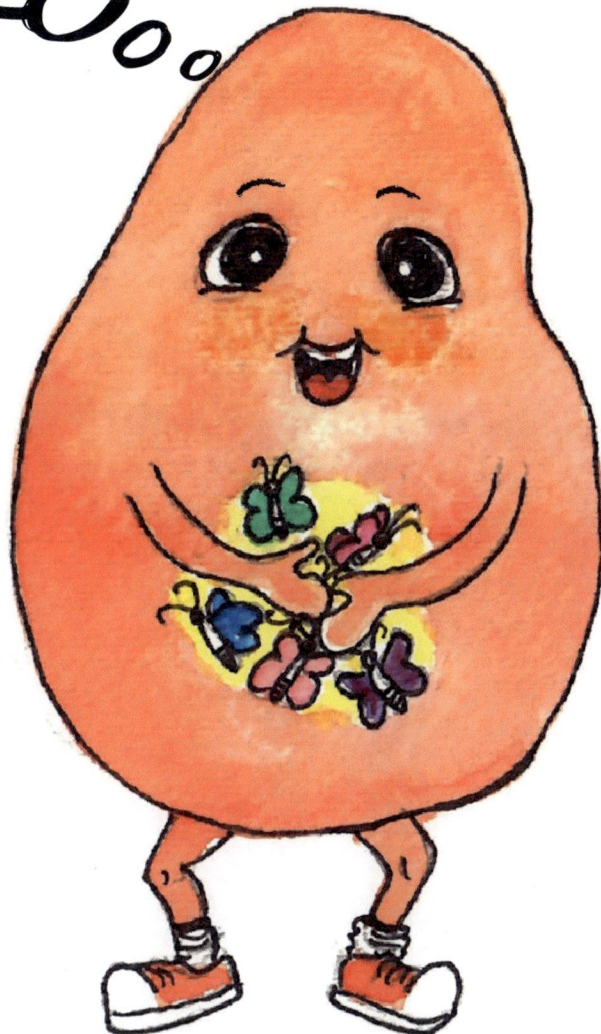

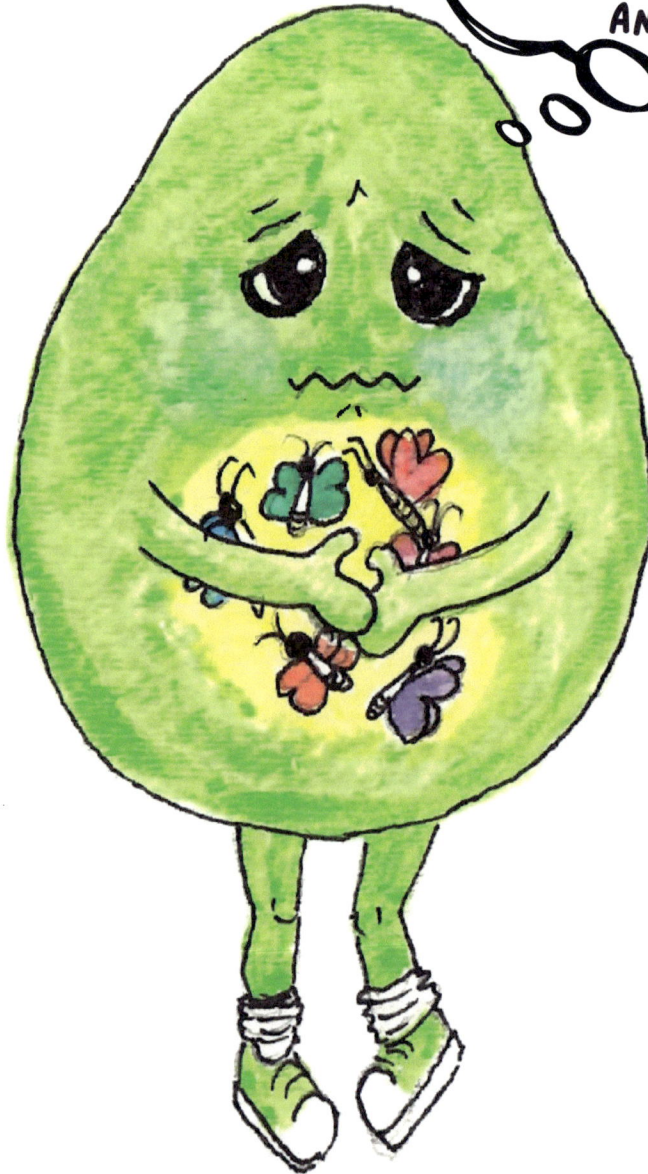

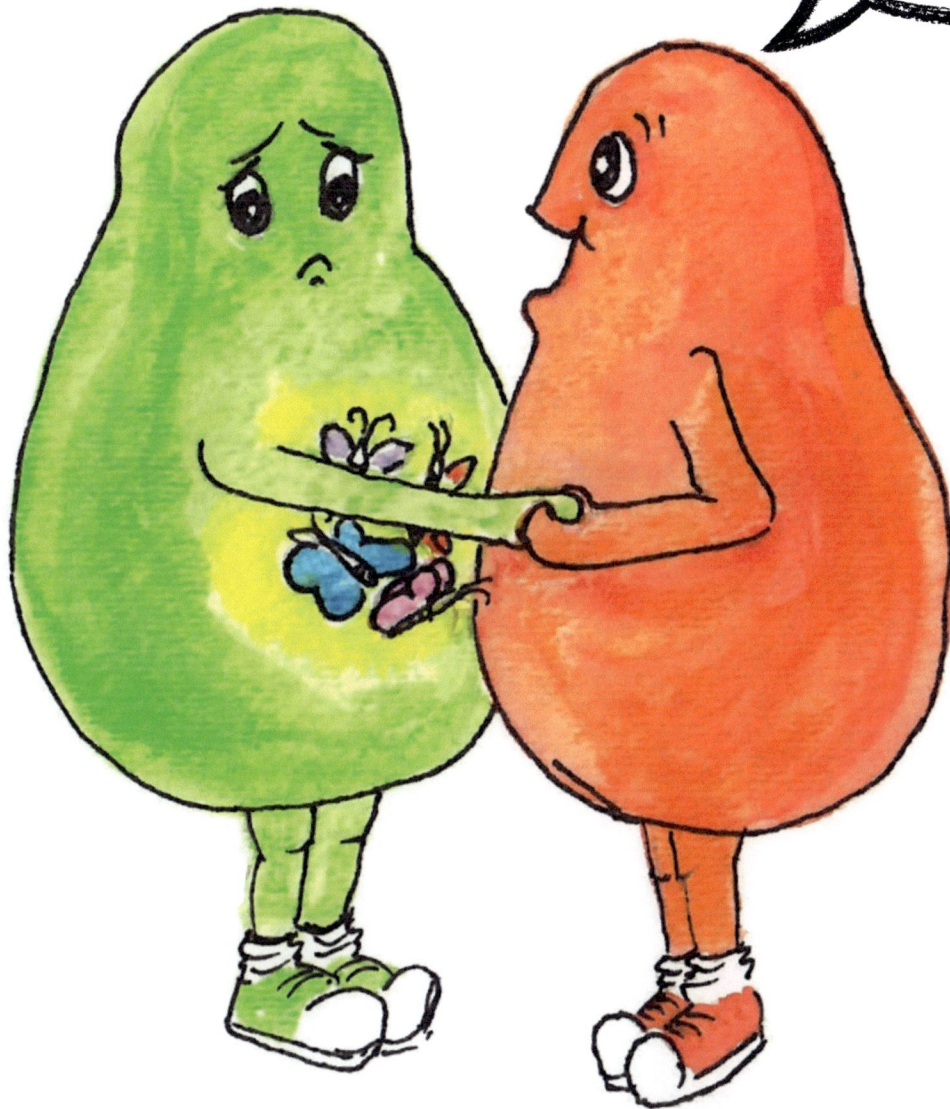

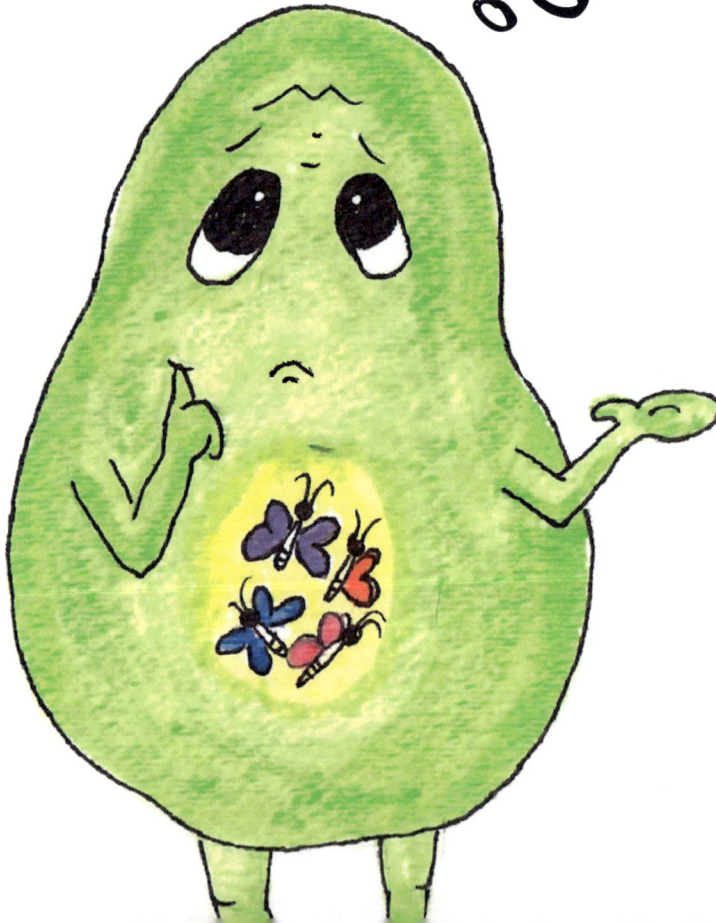

SO ARLO RUNS TO THE GARDEN, FEELING BAD.
ZUG LOOKS AWAY, CONFUSED AND SAD.

ZUG SCURRIES OFF TO THE PLAY STRUCTURE, ALONE.

A BUTTERFLY COMES OUT OF ZUG'S TUMMY, WHOA!

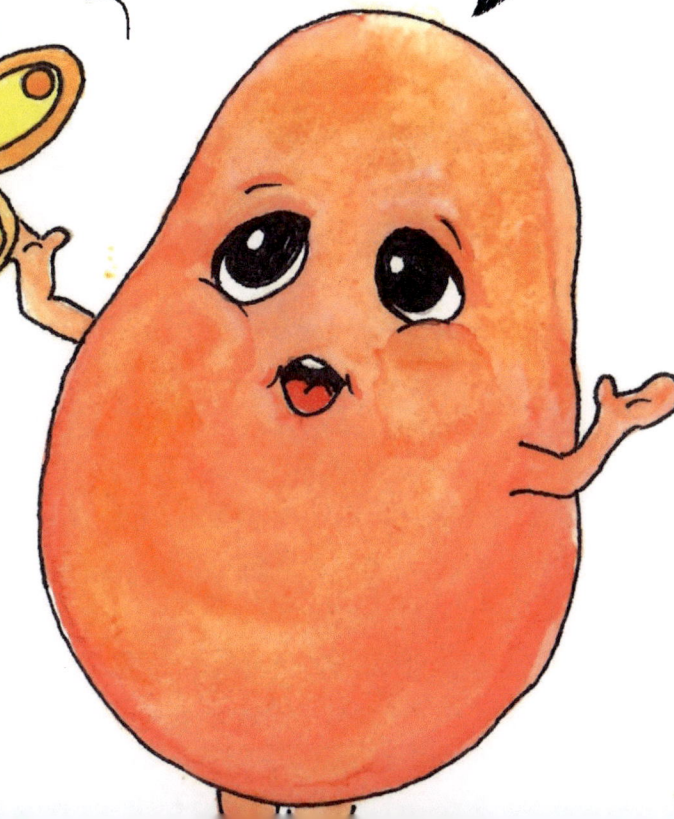

"OH, YOU THINK SO?", ASKED FLUTTERBYE.
"HOW DO YOU KNOW? CAN YOU TELL ME WHY?"

"WHEN I GAVE ARLO A HUG, THEY RAN AWAY.
WHEN I HELD THEIR HAND, THEY DID NOT STAY!"

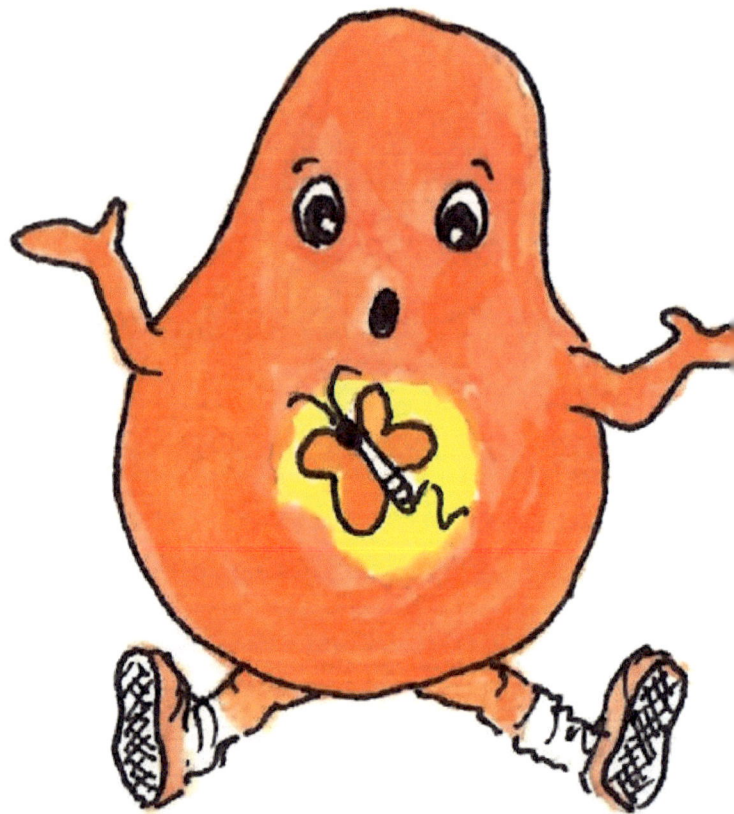

"OH! I AM SO SORRY, ZUG.
DID YOU ASK YOUR FRIEND
IF THEY LIKE HUGS?"

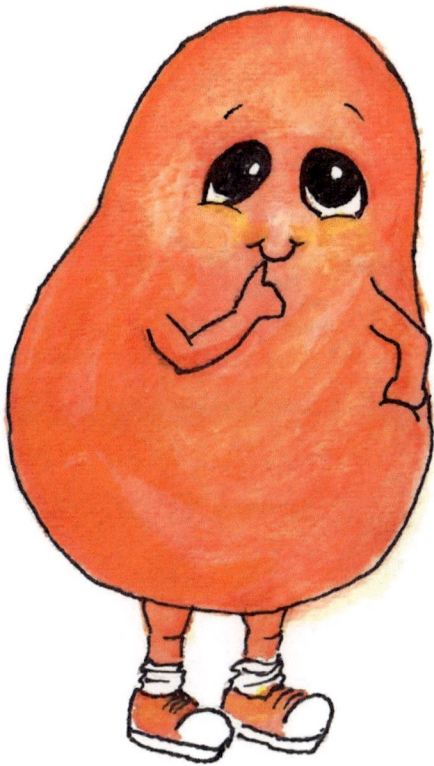

"NO, I DID NOT,
I WAS SO EXCITED!
I WANTED TO HUG,
AND I COULD NOT HIDE IT."

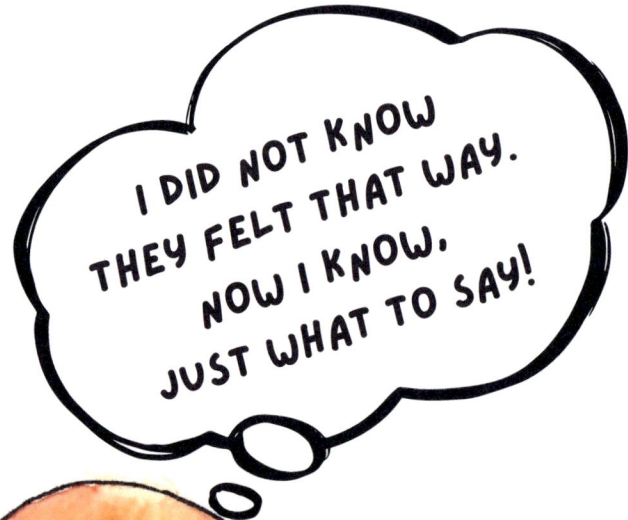

ARLO IS STILL IN THE GARDEN, ALONE.
A BUTTERFLY FLIES OUT OF THEIR TUMMY,
WHOA!

ZUG WANTED HUGS
AND TO HOLD MY HAND.
I DON'T THINK IT FELT GOOD.
I DON'T UNDERSTAND.

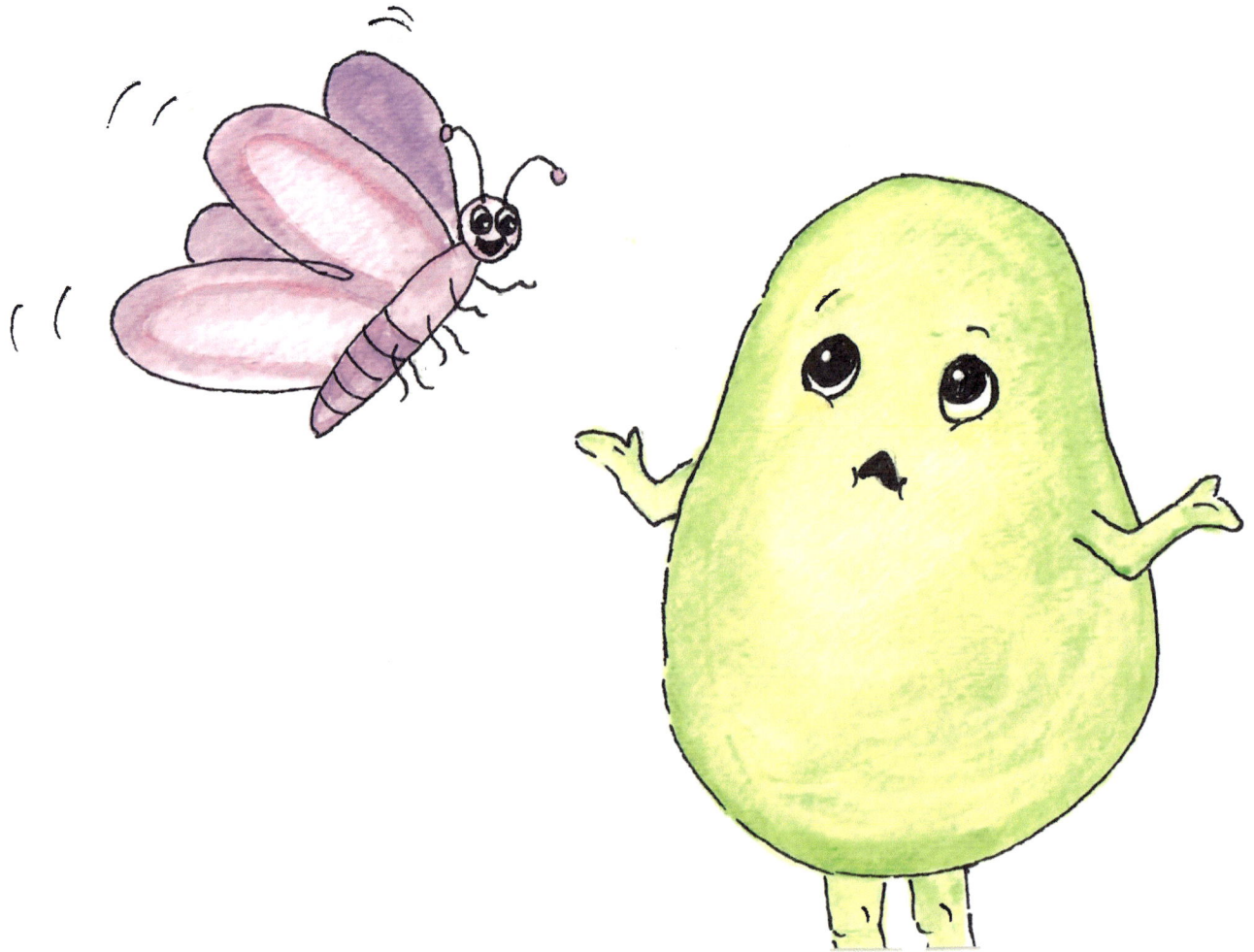

"SOMETIMES, WE DON'T WANT TO BE TOUCHED. WE CAN TELL OUR FRIENDS IF IT IS TOO MUCH."

"I WANT TO TELL THEM, BUT I DON'T KNOW HOW. I AM NOT FEELING SO GOOD RIGHT NOW."

"HELLO ARLO, ARE YOU OKAY?"

"I DON'T FEEL GOOD, ZUG, I MUST SAY."

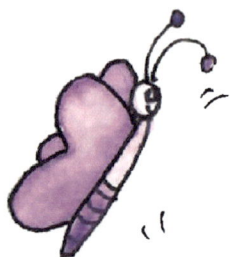

THE END

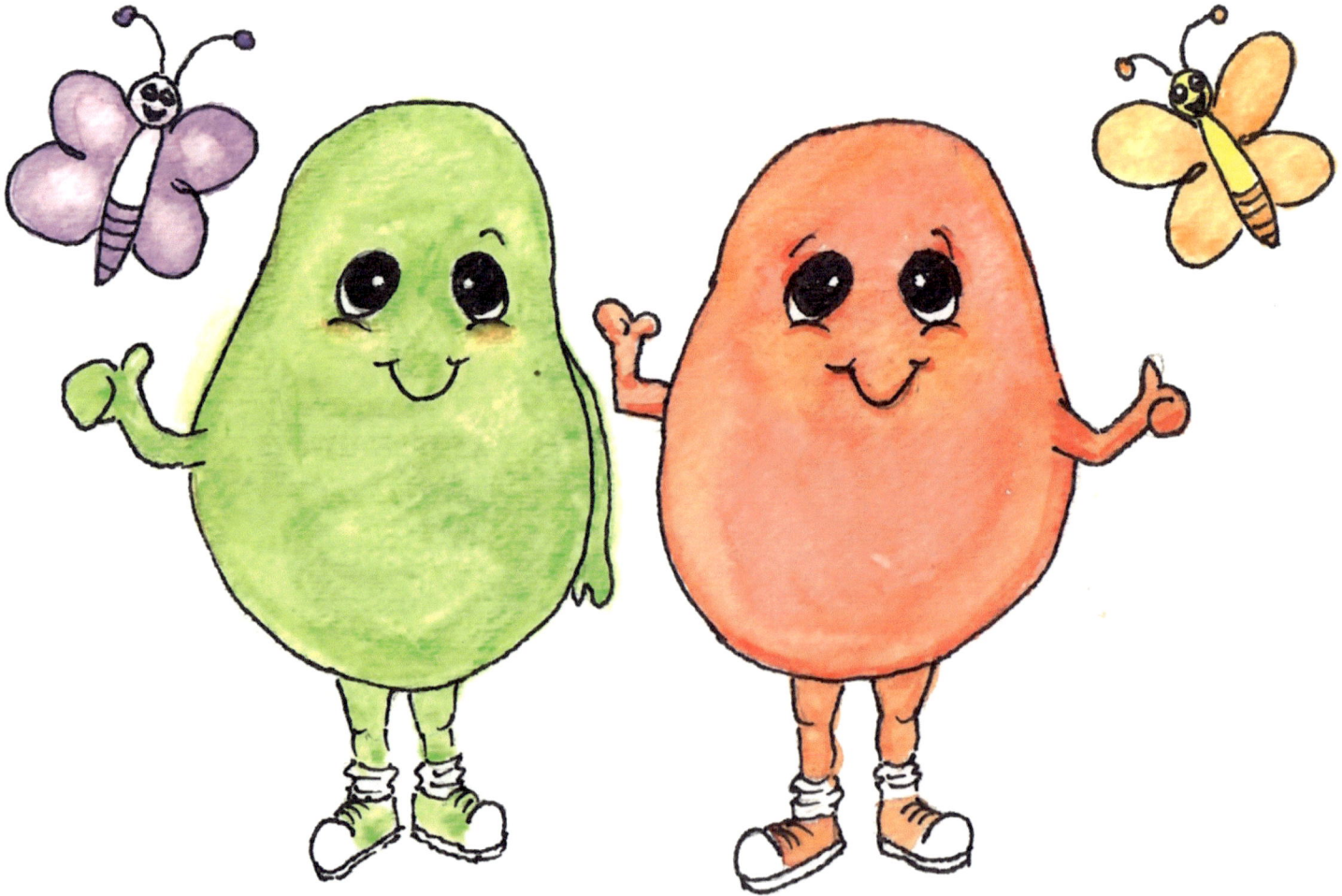

BACKGROUND

CHLOE MESHEL-WOOD RECEIVED HER MASTERS IN SOCIAL WORK AT UCLA, AND IS NOW A MEDICAL SOCIAL WORKER AT UCLA MATTEL CHILDREN'S HOSPITAL. HER GREATEST PASSION IS UNDERSTANDING HUMAN EMOTION. SHE BASES HER PRACTICE ON UNDERSTANDING THAT EACH HUMAN EXPERIENCES THEIR ENVIRONMENT DIFFERENTLY DUE TO THEIR UNIQUE INTERSECTIONALITIES.

ILLUSTRATOR OF THIS BOOK, LAURA MESHEL (CHLOE'S MOM), IS A 2ND GRADE TEACHER AT GRANT ELEMENTARY SCHOOL IN SANTA MONICA. CHLOE AND LAURA OFTEN DISCUSS CONFLICTS IN THE CLASSROOM WITH A PSYCHOSOCIAL PERSPECTIVE. CHLOE WAS INSPIRED TO WRITE THIS BOOK WHEN LAURA EXPLAINED A CONFLICT INVOLVING CONSENT AT SCHOOL.

CHLOE COULD NOT FIND ANY CHILDREN'S BOOKS ENCOURAGING CHILDREN TO USE THEIR OWN AUTONOMY TO DECIDE IF AN INTERACTION FEELS "RIGHT" OR "GOOD". THE STORY OF ARLO AND ZUG BLOSSOMED, WITH HOPES OF STARTING DEEPER CONVERSATIONS ABOUT CONSENT WITH CHILDREN.

Made in United States
Troutdale, OR
02/11/2025